Editor's Note

Will never stop providing the best content related to Business and many other topics in a magazine.

It is my commitment and the entire Business Insight Magazine team to always provide the latest and most substantive content on the local and international because we believe our readers deserve the best.

Anil Anwar
Editor In Chief

Take a closer look at the latest issue 19 of Business Insight Magazine. This issue is packed with insightful features and expert advice for business owners and entrepreneurs.

Our issue includes a wealth of helpful tips and advice for business owners, from building a personal brand to surviving a recession.

And don't miss our special section on advertising, packed with advice for businesses looking to reach new customers. Whether you're just starting out or you're a seasoned business owner, this issue 18 of Business Insight Magazine has something for you.

BUSSINESS INSIGHT MAGAZINE

www.businessinsightmag.com

JEWELZ YOGA llc

Ready to assist you achieving your body goals

Workout With

JEWEL

Professional Yoga Trainer

Feel free to contact me with any questions or inquiries.
Join Jewelz Yoga tribe by joining one of many individual, group, personalized to your event and specialty yoga classes.

Together we will make the world a more beautiful place...
one yoga breath at a time

BOOK MORE SESSIONS
SAVE MORE MONEY

JEWELZYOGA@GMAIL.COM

Make Appointment
www.jewelzyoga.com

BUSINESS INSIGHT MAGAZINE

ADVERTISING

WAYS TO PROMOTE YOUR BUSINESS

Since YEAR FOUNDED, we've been dedicated to crafting creative strategies that shape and ignite brand acceleration. From concept ideation to execution, BUSINESS INSIGHT MAGAZINE is here to help you every step of the way.

Business Insight Magazine can connect you to one of the United States largest audiences Advertise with Business Insight Magazine and unlock thousands of new customers, grow your business and increase profits.

Advertise in Business Insight Magazine and boost your business.

Let's get started with your ad, contact us today!

www.businessinsightmag.com

BUSINESS INSIGHT MAGAZINE
ISSUE 19 | FEB 2023

CONTENTS

EXCLUSIVE!

07 — 10 QUESTIONS WITH **EVA SYKORA**
www.tantra-expert.com

15 — BEAUTY AND NAKED BODIES
By Jackie Mandis

24 — SELF CARE IS SELF-LOVE
By Nikki Fielding

30 — READY TO LAUNCH?
TOP 10 STARTUP IDEAS FOR 2023

37 — UNLEASH YOUR INNER SEX SYMBOL
WITH THESE ENTREPRENEUR TIPS

43 — GET READY FOR VALENTINE'S DAY:
TIPS TO MAKE IT SEXY

51 — THROUGH TANTRA TO SEXOLOGY
WHY COMBINING SCIENCE WITH SPIRITUALITY ALLOWS YOU TO BETTER UNDERSTAND YOUR SEXUALITY?

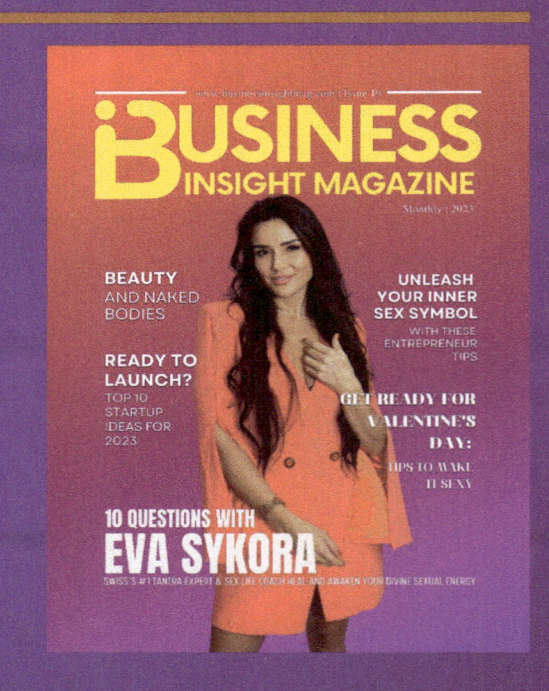

CHIEF EXECUTIVE OFFICER : ANIL ANWAR | **EDITOR-IN-CHIEF:** ANIL ANWAR | **EDITORIAL TEAM:** SABA JENN , MARY JONES

MAGAZINE INTERIOR DESIGN: SABA JENN | **PUBLISHER:** CAPITOL TIMES MEDIA

Website
www.businessinsightmag.com

Email
magazines@capitoltimesmedia.com

ISSN
Print: 2771-5159
Digital: 2771-5167

BOMBSHELL

EAU DE PARFUM

Bold & Iconic
Sparkling and fresh, our number-one fragrance is a timeless mix of fresh-cut, exotic flowers and afternoon sun.

Purple Passion Fruit • Shangri-la Peony
Vanilla Orchid

SCAN ME

prime video
THE LORD OF THE RINGS
THE RINGS OF POWER
WATCH NOW | NEW SERIES
SCAN ME

BUSINESS INSIGHT MAGAZINE | ISSUE 19 | 2023

PAGE 07

10 Questions With
EVA SYKORA

WWW.TANTRA-EXPERT.COM

Anwar: We have guest this month Eva Sykora, She is Sex & Life Coach.

Eva, Can you give us some background on how you found your passion in Tantra?

Eva Sykora: Sharing and teaching Tantra is today my life's mission. For me it all started with the need to heal a childhood's trauma as, as so many kids, I have been sexually abused at the age of 5. This first negative experience forbad me to feel pleasure in my body, in other words to experience orgasm. But even worse, I suffered constant pain in my intimate area - for almost 2 years! At this stage, I had to face the limitations of conventional medicine and was therefore forced to look for alternatives. After opening to different parallel medicines, I finally had the chance to take part when I was 19 to my first tantra training for women: for the first time I could feel my body: I was alive! It immediately became my passion: I literally fell in love with Tantra. Later I understood that is not only about Tantra and body-energetic work but that is important to work also on subconscious mind and emotions. So I created my own FORMULA: 4 ELEMENTS UNLISHING PERSONAL AND SEXUAL POWER (body, mind, emotions and energy). It has been the pivotal element of my healing process. And after learning it for myself, it became evidence to share it to provide the same help that I could receive. I had my mission! Today, I am convinced that through our personal stories, what we have experienced on our skin, we are able to understand and help more effectively other people experiencing the same problems.

Anwar: There is a great deal of instant gratification in our society today. Do you think that this also applies to sexual relationships?

Eva Sykora: As immediateness became a core value for our modern society, it also influencing our sexual relationship. People and especially teenagers or young adults feel the need to immediately "consume" the relationship and experience positions and practices similar to those promoted by pornography. This ego driven sexuality is unfortunately the driver of frustrations. The approach I promote goes against this tendency: quality and pleasure require patience! It starts by knowing your own body. Then you should know each other body to know where and how to caress. The orgasmic state will only be reached if the sexual energy is increased and expanded by breath, sound and right movements.. Concretely, at least one hour of foreplay activity including deep eye contact, caressing and intense and increasing sensuality will create the arousal and the sexual energy to bring the lovers to orgasm before and during the penetration.

Anwar: What is the main difference between "conventional" and tantric sex? Is there a greater exploration of the senses?

Eva Sykora: Tantric sex implies a deeper connection between the partners, starting by everyone deeply connected with his / her own body. The tantric sex involves that lovers have awaken their energetic systems. They can therefore have higher vibrations allowing more intense pleasure. Consequently, by being more connected to their bodies and to each other, lovers will definitely explore further their senses.

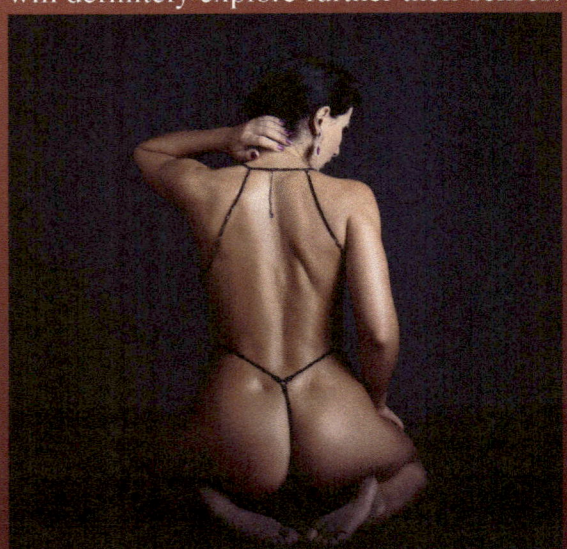

Anwar: What other pleasures can help prolong sex and pleasure are we omitting?

Eva Sykora: Breathing is a very underestimated activity; here I am referring to conscious breathing. It increases but also prolongs the pleasure. This can be easily experienced by, for instance, starting the sexual intercourse by breathing deeply while watching the partner in the eyes. It might sound simple, but you will be surprised by the results! Tantra brings of course many techniques increasing the sexual energy and pleasure by caressing the right way at the right places. Self-pleasuring increases the quality of the sexual relationship allowing you to be more connected to your body. Self-pleasuring is not about masturbating but literally making love to yourself: this is the secret to make better love: starting with yourself!

Anwar: What about the positions, is there any more suitable for those who want to delay ejaculation?

Eva Sykora: Probably many have already experienced that laying on the back can delay ejaculation as the blood pressure is reduced. Important is to share that the man should still be active as if he is only "guided" by the motions of his partner this can still trigger premature ejaculation due to the lack of control.

Another position allowing men to control better the ejaculation is when both lovers sit in lotus flower position. But it is important to underline that tantra is primarily not about learning new positions but the golden nugget is to increase and extend the sexual energy, then to awaken body and to connect with ourselves and soul.

Anwar: What actually led you to tantra and why did you decide to stay on that path?

Eva Sykora: As earlier mentioned, Tantra allowed to me heal and it gave me also the capacity to help others… But it also allowed me to discover my sexual potential. With my body being awaken, I could become multi-orgasmic meaning that all my cells can vibrate of pleasure. Tantra has awaken my consciousness, chakras and energetic system. Tantra is for me the source of vital energy and creativity. Tantra has literally open my heart and feel connected with ONES!

Anwar: Do most of your clients tend to be men or women, and what is their average age? How old was your youngest client and how old was your oldest client?

Eva Sykora: My clients are 60% men and 40% women: their average age is about 45 with a large diversity between 25 to 75 years old.

Anwar: What is the difference between sensuality vs. sexuality?

Eva Sykora: From my point of view, sexuality refers to animality, it is generated by our instinct to procreate; this is a natural process including arousal, penetration, and ejaculation. To cut it short and please excuse my French: sexuality can be pictured as rabbit-fucking while sensuality is about using all senses, being playful and creative, breathing, moving, and connecting deeply with yourself and your partner.

Anwar: How can a deeper spiritual understanding of sexual pleasure lead to self-empowerment and soul connection?

Eva Sykora: While conventional sex triggers usually focus only on sexual organs, extended sexual energy awakens all chakras. This awakening will also allow you to connect with your heart and your soul, freeing up yourself of the demanding ego. Being in command of the

4 elements (body, mind, soul and energy) and knowing who you really are and what you really want, will naturally lead to better decisions and actions: soul driven rather than ego commanded!

Anwar: What exciting things do you have planned for the future and how can people who are interested get involved?

Eva Sykora: We have just entered the age of Aquarius and this age will be different from the previous one. It is made up of much more subtle and higher frequencies. Those who do not accompany this outer dimensional shift with an inner dimensional shift will experience suffering, frustration, and much confusion. Therefore, I am planning to extend my offer with a stronger online presence. This is for me an important evolution allowing me to reach and to help a larger number of people and to leverage these higher frequencies as I have developed a practice combining 4 elements my FORMULA: 4 ELEMENTS UNLISHING PERSONAL AND SEXUAL POWER (body, emotions, mind and energy) online.

New project (additional from sexual healing) is concretely propose a guided support to address:

- Handling pain after separation
- Managing anxiousness and stress within the relationship
- Eliminating the fear to be abandoned, fear to be alone
- Getting away from toxic relationship
- Recognizing manipulation and stopping manipulating
- Reborning after the end of the relationship
- Regrowing self-esteem after a separation
- Being more self-confident in sexual relationship

BUSINESS INSIGHT MAGAZINE | ISSUE 19 | 2023   PAGE 13

CONTACT ME

- 🌐 www.tantra-expert.com
- Ⓕ www.facebook.com/evasykoralatuarinascita
- 📷 @Eva_Sykora

Try Exercise with Eva
www.tantra-expert.com/en/excercises-access/

JEWELZ YOGA llc

Ready to assist you achieving your body goals

Workout With

JEWEL
Professional Yoga Trainer

Feel free to contact me with any questions or inquiries.
Join Jewelz Yoga tribe by joining one of many individual, group, personalized to your event and specialty yoga classes.

Together we will make the world a more beautiful place...
one yoga breath at a time

BOOK MORE SESSIONS
SAVE MORE MONEY

JEWELZYOGA@GMAIL.COM

Make Appointment
www.jewelzyoga.com

BUSINESS INSIGHT MAGAZINE | ISSUE 19 | 2023
PAGE 15

BEAUTY
AND NAKED BODIES

You may not think of beauty and naked bodies when you think of Corporate America, but that is all about to change.

More and more corporations are realizing the importance of beauty and naked bodies in the workplace. They are recognizing the value of a positive body image and the benefits that it can bring to employees and the company as a whole.

Naked bodies have been shown to increase productivity, creativity, and morale. They can also help to reduce stress levels and promote team unity. In short, they can help to improve the overall work environment.

So, if you are looking for a new job, or if you are simply interested in what is happening in the world of Corporate America, keep an eye out for businesses that are championing beauty and naked bodies. It is a movement that is sure to grow in the years ahead.

BUSINESS INSIGHT MAGAZINE | ISSUE 19 | 2023   PAGE 17

THE IMPACT OF BEAUTY ON CORPORATE AMERICA

What is considered beautiful affects how people are perceived in the corporate world.

Your appearance is extremely important in the corporate world. You need to be dressed well and look professional at all times. You also need to be thin and fit, as this is what is considered to be beautiful.

If you do not meet these standards, you will be at a disadvantage. You will be seen as less competent and less qualified than your peers, and you will have a harder time getting ahead in your career.

BUSINESS INSIGHT MAGAZINE | ISSUE 19 | 2023   PAGE 18

AN INCREASE IN HALF NAKED BODIES IN THE WORKPLACE

You have probably seen more naked bodies in the workplace lately.

There has been a recent trend of businesses embracing the half naked body. From clothing-optional offices to nude yoga classes, corporations are trying to create a more relaxed and open work environment.

While some people may see this as a step forward in terms of body positivity, others see it as a cheap ploy to get people to work harder. They argue that by exposing employees to other people's naked bodies, businesses are creating an atmosphere of sexualization and objectification.

What do you think?

APPROACHES TO PROFESSIONALISM AND BODY IMAGE

So, what are your thoughts on the matter?

It can be difficult to maintain a professional image when your employer is asking you to tone down your natural look or to go against your personal beliefs. However, with a bit of effort, it is possible to find an approach to professionalism that works for you.

Some people may find it helpful to have a strict dress code, while others may prefer to be more flexible. It is important to find what works best for you and to be comfortable with your appearance.

In addition, it is important to be comfortable with your body and to not feel ashamed of your nakedness. Remember that you are professional, regardless of how much or how little clothing you are wearing.

APPROACHES TO PROFESSIONALISM AND BODY IMAGE

The idea of acceptable dress and beauty standards in the workplace is something that many people are exploring.

It's no longer a matter of simply slipping on your best business suit or your favorite blouse and skirt combo.

You must now consider what is appropriate, and even acceptable, for your body type and for the environment.

It's important to be aware of how you are presenting yourself to the world at all times, especially on the job.

Anything from the length of your skirt to the depth of your V-neck can potentially be seen as unprofessional and, depending on where you work, could even result in disciplinary action.

Make sure that you are conscious of these standards at all times so that you keep your job instead of losing it over something as insignificant as which clothes you choose to wear.

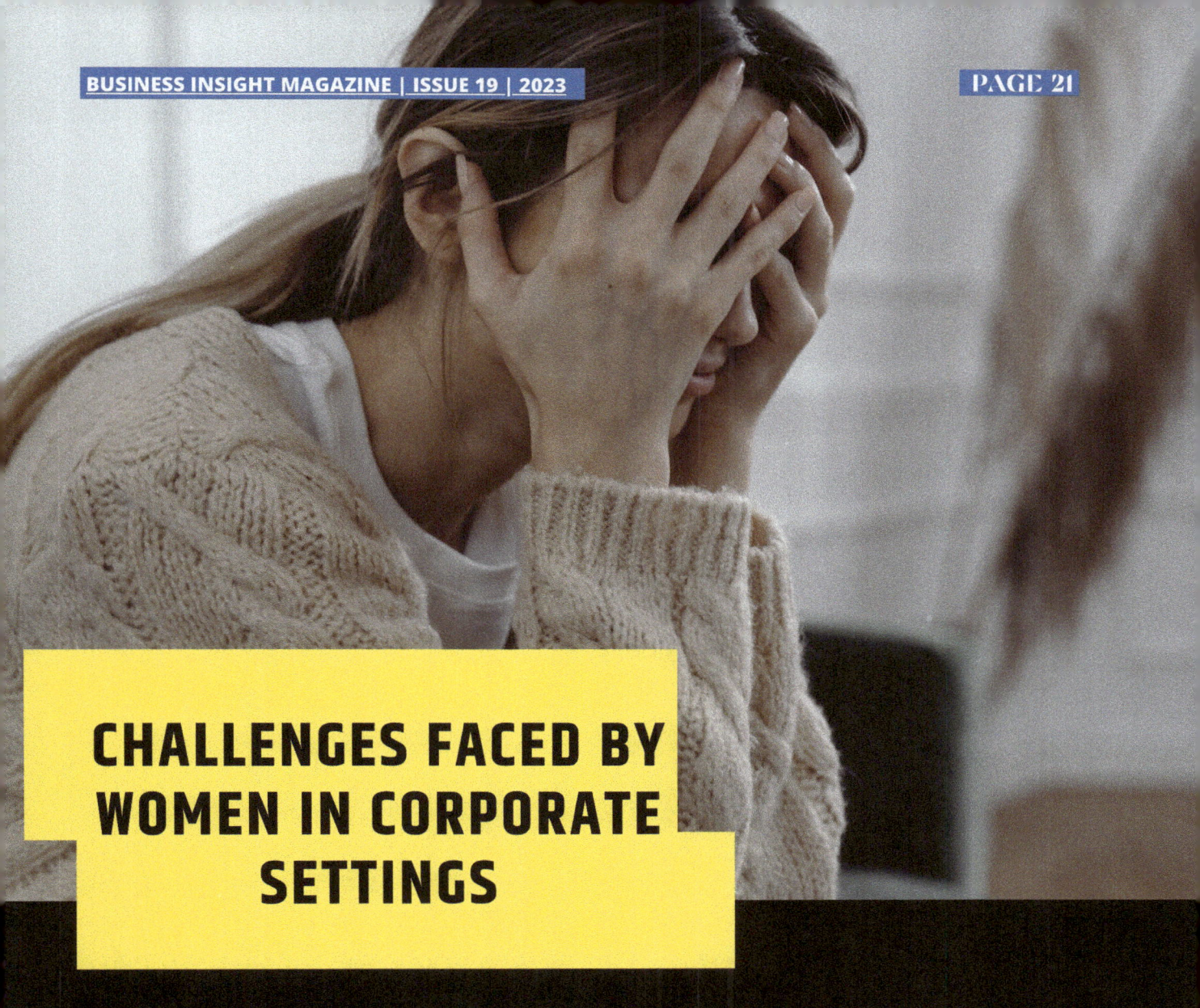

CHALLENGES FACED BY WOMEN IN CORPORATE SETTINGS

You may be surprised to learn that female business professionals in corporate America may not feel comfortable wearing clothing that is revealing or "too sexy". This is because there are still many cultural expectations surrounding what is considered appropriate office attire.

Women can often be judged and harassed for their clothing choices, even if it is something as innocuous as wearing a dress with a plunging neckline.

Additionally, some women do not feel comfortable engaging in conversations about beauty and naked bodies at the office.

There are still some professional settings where such topics are seen as off-limits, and women can

LOOKING TOWARD CHANGE AND EQULITY

You can see the shift in expectations when it comes to beauty and naked bodies in corporate America.

Companies are recognizing that employees should be treated equally regardless of gender, race, sexual orientation, and physical appearance.

Workplaces are taking steps to promote progress and equality by introducing diversity and inclusion initiatives.

This includes initiatives such as improving workplace policies and procedures, creating Mentor Spaces for minorities, having more flexible working practices for people with different needs, and encouraging a better perception of beauty within the business environment.

These changes will take time, but they have the potential to have a lasting impact on how employees view their own bodies and their place within the corporate world.

CONCLUSION

The business of beauty is booming, and corporate America is taking notice. Across the country, major brands are launching campaigns and initiatives focused on body positivity and diversity. Naked bodies are being celebrated, and the industry is finally starting to recognize the importance of inclusivity.

Why is this change happening now? Perhaps it's because society is finally starting to recognize that beauty comes in all shapes and sizes. Or maybe it's because consumers are demanding more diversity in the products they buy. Whatever the reason, it's clear that the landscape of beauty is changing, and corporate America is leading the charge.

SELF CARE IS SELF-LOVE

By Nikki Fielding

What better time than February – the month of Valentine's Day - to celebrate our love for ourselves?

This may seem counter intuitive as the holiday is surrounded by commercialism and the need to buy things to show others how much we love them.

However, we can only meet another as deeply as we have met ourselves. The more we love ourselves the deeper our connections and relationships with others and the world around us becomes. Self-care is self-love.

What exactly is self-care? Often our mind first goes to things like treating ourselves to a massage, spa treatments, vacations, or buying ourselves that thing that we've been wanting and we may tell ourselves (true or not) I can't afford self-care.

I need to spend that time making money, taking care of my loved ones, or doing any one of the endless things on that to do list…there's truly no end to things that may feel more important than caring for ourselves.

Self-care does not equate to self-indulgence, pampering, or being selfish. But rather taking care of ourselves so we can be healthy, happy, do our job, help care for others, and do the things we need or want to accomplish on any given day.

It's the practice of taking care of our own health and wellbeing using the knowledge and information available to us. Thanks to modern technology there is no shortage of available information at our fingertips!

While technology is wonderful and makes it easier to access information, communicate with people around the world, and be productive from nearly any location, it also takes a toll.

Pings, alerts, rings, and notifications can shift our focus in a way that may lead to long-lasting difficulties with paying attention.

Struggling to pay attention frequently leads to poorer performance on academic, professional, or personal tasks. Researchers in France and the UK found that frequent media multitasking contributes to diminished gray matter in region of our brain where attention control resides.

Sadly, the impact to our brain doesn't end here. It can also wear out the pleasure center of our brains by overstimulating dopamine making our brain's pleasure center less responsive to other enjoyable experiences like eating a delicious meal, reading a good book, or having a conversation with someone we care about.

Both falling down that proverbial online rabbit-hole as well as the blue light interferes with our circadian rhythm and may cause reduced sleep. It may contribute to one limiting physical activity and can even hinder our memories. The "Google Effect" – the tendency to not feel the need to store information in our brains as it is accessible with the click of a button - is the phenomenon of decreased long-term and working memory.

Some researchers believe that cognitive conditions like Alzheimer's could be associated with failing to maximize our cognitive capacities and are alarmed by the
Google Effect and its potential impact on these conditions.

Even in the modern world and using modern technology, we can make time for self-care. In fact, it's more essential than ever. Prioritizing our needs - mind, body, and spirit – allows us to better cope with daily stressors.

There is a global epidemic of anxiety and depression. Everybody feels it. We can't help but feel it as we are all connected and all one. A common sign of feeling anxious and overwhelmed is the bunny rabbit effect. This is a term I've made up (as far as I know).

Do you find yourself hopping around from one task to another and feeling scattered and overwhelmed?

You may have plenty of energy and motivation but can't seem to focus and channel it into getting important things done or seeing certain tasks through to completion?

Ever felt like a little bunny rabbit happily eating some grass and then…something catches your eye or comes to your mind and you are immediately distracted and switch gears to another task?

Not only are there more things to accomplish than ever, but we are also living through crazy times. Intense world events, the aging of the global population and rise of chronic disease, uncertain economic times. Combined with the near constant use of technology, it's no wonder we are distracted! Learning to focus our attention and develop the mental fitness needed to slow down and focus on our own needs helps build resilience.

Resilience is made up of five pillars: Self-Awareness, Mindfulness, Self-Care, Positive Relationships, and Purpose.

Resiliency positively affects life satisfaction and psychological distress through its impact on our self-esteem. They mutually affect each other as we learn to extend more compassion to, and ultimately feel better about ourselves as beings, we are able to better withstand the sometimes crazy roller-coaster we call life.

And begin to feel worthy of compassion, grace, kindness, rest, and having our needs met by ourselves and others. Self-care boils down to knowing our worth and giving our mind, body, and spirit what it needs to thrive.

We must fully recognize our inherent worth: the intrinsic worth for simply existing as your beautiful and perfectly imperfect and unique self. So many have been conditioned to link our worth to results, accomplishments, performance, or outcomes but it's truly a divine gift bestowed to each of us. We simply need to remember that we were given that gift and learn to truly believe and embody its essence.

Self-care involves choosing to take action every day towards being the healthiest, happiest, and highest versions of ourselves. It can be as simple as: taking a step back, asking for help, spending time alone, putting yourself first, asking for what you need, staying at home to rest, saying no, or forgiving yourself for being a perfectly imperfect being like everyone else. There are 8 primary areas of self-care: physical, psychological, emotional, social, professional, environmental, and financial. And endless opportunities to develop our knowledge in these areas and carve out space to apply this knowledge in our lives. The only thing holding you back is you. Learn to silence that voice that says you don't matter, you'll take care of yourself after (insert reason), or there's other more important things to dedicate your time and energy to. Set yourself up for success and start small! 2 minutes of meditation is better than none. 10 minutes of physical activity is better than living a sedentary lifestyle. Making a simple healthy swap in your diet to incorporate more nourishing foods or less inflammatory foods helps build the motivation and discipline to continue to make more choices that honor the highest version of yourself.

SOME FREE OR VERY ACCESSIBLE IDEAS TO INCORPORATE MORE SELF-CARE INTO YOUR DAILY AND WEEKLY ROUTINE INCLUDE:

- Reading books
- Practicing Meditation
- Getting in a good workout
- Spending time in nature
- Practicing good sleep hygiene by limiting screen time in the hours leading up to bed and keeping a consistent schedule for falling asleep and waking
- Closing your eyes and allowing your body to move and sway to music without thinking about how it looks — only how it feels
- Journaling about your goals, reviewing your day, or how you are truly feeling inside
- Making healthier diet choices to fuel our bodies
- Enjoying a cup of tea
- Taking a digital detox for an hour, day, or even week
- Treating yourself to an Epsom salt bath
- Defining your core values and better aligning your life with them
- Communicating your emotional needs
- Decluttering or organizing your space
- Finally getting to that doctor's appointment you've been putting off
- Investing in a course, masterclass, or working with a coach who specializes in an area of self-care you could use more support and guidance

For those ready to deepen their self-care practice working with someone like me who specializes in this is often life changing. There's a reason the life, health, and wellness coaching industry is one of the fastest growing markets and predicted to continue to grow exponentially throughout this decade. We learn best through experience. And investing in those who have experience and can share their wisdom, what works, as well as the endless mistakes they made along the way while learning can help us level up and apply this wisdom to our lives and relationships on a larger scale.

Consider the difference between knowledge and wisdom. The primary difference between the two is that wisdom involves a healthy dose of perspective and the ability to make sound judgments about a subject while knowledge is simply knowing. Anyone can become knowledgeable on a subject through any variety of methods.

Wisdom requires more understanding and the ability to determine which facts are relevant in certain situations.

It takes knowledge and applies it with discernment based on experience, evaluation and lessons learned. Self-love is the revolution. We have been programmed to put ourselves last. To consider investing time, money, and energy into taking care of ourselves as "unessential." You can't pour from an empty cup.

Just like the spiel at the beginning of any flight instructs us in the event of an emergency to put our own oxygen mask on first before assisting others around us, you should be your own highest priority. In an effort to better serve yourself, those who rely on you, and the world at large. Wishing you all a beautiful month honoring your love for self and others and fully feeling into your own infinite worth.

To work with me or for more tips on self-care and deepening your alignment mind, body, and spirit

follow me on socials:

LinkedIn:
https://www.linkedin.com/in/nikkifielding
Facebook: Nikki Fielding
Instagram: @nfielding03

BUSINESS INSIGHT MAGAZINE | ISSUE 19 | 2023

PAGE 30

READY TO LAUNCH?

TOP 10 STARTUP IDEAS FOR 2023

2023 is shaping up to be an incredible year for business. With so many new and innovative ideas floating around, there's no telling what could take off and become the next big thing.

But don't worry, we're here to help you get ahead of the curve. We've compiled a list of the hottest startup ideas of 2023, so you can be sure to stay ahead of the trends and launch a business that's sure to succeed.

From sustainable fashion to plant-based food, these are the businesses you need to be on the lookout for in the coming year. So what are you waiting for? Start planning your next big venture now!

What Kinds of Businesses Are on the Rise?

As we inch closer to 2023, it's time to start thinking about the types of businesses that will be on the rise in the coming year. So what kinds of businesses should you consider launching in 2023?

Here are some ideas to get you started:

1.Health and fitness: With the rise of wellness and healthy living, it's no surprise that health and fitness businesses are on the rise. From gyms and yoga studios to meal delivery services and weight loss programs, there is a lot of opportunity in this niche.

2.Tech startups: As technology continues to evolve, so does the tech startup industry. If you have a innovative idea for a new app or software, 2023 is the year to launch your business.

3.Home services: More and more people are opting to stay at home rather than go out to eat or spend money on services. This provides a lot of opportunity for home-based businesses, such as home-cleaning services, pet-sitting, or personal chef services.

4.Foodie businesses: With the foodie culture on the rise, it's no surprise that food-related businesses are doing well. From artisanal bakeries to gourmet catering companies, there is a lot of room for culinary creativity in this industry.

5.E-commerce businesses: Thanks to the growth of online shopping, e-commerce businesses are continuing to thrive. If you have a good idea for an online store, 2023 is the year to launch your business.

How to Spot and Capitalize on Emerging Trends

So what's hot in 2023? Here are a few trends to watch out for and capitalize on:

1. Eco-friendly businesses: We're seeing a growing trend of eco-friendly and sustainable businesses. Consumers are becoming more and more conscious of their impact on the planet, and are looking for businesses that align with their values. If you can tap into this trend, you're in for big success!

2. Health and fitness: The health and fitness industry is booming, and there's no sign of it slowing down anytime soon. This is a great industry to get into if you're passionate about helping people get healthy and stay fit.

3. Food and beverage: With the rise of foodie culture, it's no surprise that the food and beverage industry is trending upwards. People are always looking for new and innovative ways to tantalize their taste buds, so if you're a culinary genius, this is the industry for you!

The Benefits of Starting a Business in 2023

So you're thinking of starting a business? That's AWESOME! Starting your own business is one of the most rewarding things you can do in life. Not only do you get to be your own boss, but you also get to call the shots and set your own hours.

But before you launch your business, it's important to do your research and make sure you're launching a business that's on trend. That's why we've put together a list of the hottest startup ideas for 2023. So whether you're into food, fashion, or technology, there's something for everyone!

So what are you waiting for? Start brainstorming now and get ready to launch your business in 2023!

3 Booming Businesses and Their Potential

Are you looking to launch your own business in 2023? In this paragraph, we'll dive into three of the most promising and innovative businesses that are gaining traction this year.

First up we have an AI-driven legal consulting

service that helps businesses find their perfect lawyer. This startup has already raised millions in venture funding, and it's no surprise why: AI-driven legal services could revolutionize the industry and save businesses time and money.

Second on our list is an online event planning site catered towards large corporate events. Thanks to its intuitive and customizable platform, this company is making it easier than ever for businesses to plan big events with ease—saving time, resources, and headaches.

Lastly, we have a subscription-based pet food delivery service that allows pet owners to enjoy the convenience of regular deliveries without having to make an extra trip to the store. With its competitive pricing and wide selection of options, this business is proving that it's a leader in the industry—and one to watch!

Where to Find Resources to Launch a New Business in 2023

When it comes to launching a new business in 2023, you may be wondering where to start. Fortunately, there are several resources available to help you get started.

If you have an idea for a business, but don't know how to put it into action, the Small Business Administration (SBA) can help. They offer up-to-date information on regulations, funding opportunities through grants and loans, and general tips on how to plan and launch your business. There are also numerous online courses available that can give you a crash course in the basics of starting a business.

Also consider reaching out to your personal and professional networks for guidance, advice, and even potential deals. You never know who might be able to help you get your business off the ground!

Strategies for Success in the Ever-Changing Business Landscape

To be a successful entrepreneur, you have to be adaptable. The business landscape is constantly changing, and what works today may not work tomorrow. That's why it's important to always be on the lookout for new opportunities and be willing to pivot your business model when necessary.

Here are a few strategies that will help you stay ahead of the curve and be successful in the ever-changing business landscape:

1. Stay up to date on industry trends.

2. Be willing to pivot your business model.

3. Be open to new opportunities.

4. Constantly innovate.

5. Build a strong team.

6. Focus on customer needs.

7. Stay lean and agile.

8. Measure your progress.

9. Stay focused and persistent.

10. Have a long-term vision.

If you can keep these things in mind, you'll be well on your way to success in the ever-changing business landscape.

prime video
THE LORD OF THE RINGS
THE RINGS OF POWER
WATCH NOW | NEW SERIES

BUSINESS INSIGHT MAGAZINE | ISSUE 19 | 2023

PAGE 37

UNLEASH YOUR INNER SEX SYMBOL

WITH THESE ENTREPRENEUR TIPS

You're sexy and you know it. But sometimes, you need a little help to unleash your inner sex symbol. Maybe you're struggling to find your personal brand or you've been stuck in the same job for too long. Heck, maybe you just need some inspiration to power through that final mile in your marathon training.

No matter what the challenge, we've got you covered. Check out our top 10 tips for making sexy entrepreneur. And trust us, these tips will help you look and feel your best—both inside and out!

Branding Yourself With Confidence

Start by branding yourself with confidence. When you walk into a room, own the space. You don't need to be loud or boisterous, but act like the person you want to become. Confidence is key, and it will show in everything you do.

Keep in mind that your brand is what people see when they look at you. It's the first impression that you make, and it's often what people remember long after meeting you. So make sure that it's one that you're proud of.

Tips on Packing Presence Into Your Pitch

You might not be able to change the way you look, but you can definitely change the way you present yourself. When you're pitching your business, make sure you pack in as much presence as you can.

Think about it this way: You're in a room full of people, and you're all competing for the same thing. The person who can project the most confidence, charisma and authority is going to be the one who comes out on top.

So how do you do that? Here are a few tips:

- Stand up straight and tall.
- Make eye contact with your audience.
- Use confident body language, like gestures and hand movements.
- Speak in a clear, concise voice.
- Pause occasionally to let your words sink in.

The Power of Dressing for Success

When it comes to dressing for success, it's not about wearing the most expensive clothes or having the perfect body. It's about feeling confident in what you're wearing and knowing that you look the part.

And that's something that anyone can achieve, whether you're an entrepreneur or not. With a bit of effort and some simple guidelines, you can step up your style and unleash your inner sex symbol.

Here are our top 10 tips for dressing like a sexy entrepreneur:

1. wear clothes that fit well

2. find your personal style and stick to it

3. dress for the occasion

4. know your body type and dress accordingly

5. choose quality over quantity

6. experiment with different looks

7. focus on the positive

8. accessorize wisely

9. be comfortable in your own skin

10. practice makes perfect

Networking for Sexy Success

Networking is another great way to move one step closer to being an ultra-sexy entrepreneur. Who doesn't love meeting new people, exchanging ideas and exploring business opportunities? Attending events, joining social media networks and setting up meetings with industry professionals are all great ways to succeed in your sexy entrepreneurial endeavors.

You never know who you could meet at these events and what information or advice they could offer you. They might have insights that can help you refine your pitch, improve your approach or point you in the right direction of financing and investor opportunities. These are all things that may help you pave the path to sexy success.

So the next time an opportunity arises where you can attend a networking event, grab it—it just might be the key ingredient needed for sexy success!

Smart Ways to Utilize Technology

Forget about the bad rap technology gets, because you can use it to your advantage to boost your inner sex symbol too. The key is to know how to leverage technology in a smart way.

First, create an online portfolio or website that highlights your work and background. You'll be surprised how much this tool can do for finding investors or clients, even if you're not trying to land any sex partners. And if you're ever in need of a bit of self-promotion, social media channels such as Twitter or Instagram are perfect for showcasing your skills and accomplishments without coming across as too boastful.

Finally, don't forget the power of video conferencing. This is the perfect way to network with people that may have an interest in your ideas or product. Just remember to let your enthusiasm shine through! By leveraging these methods, you'll quickly be on your way to becoming a sexy entrepreneur.

Creating Quality Content to Show Off Your Expertise

Whether you're on Instagram or Twitter, creating content that not only looks good but resonates with your audience is key to attracting potential partners. After all, a big part of being a sexy entrepreneur is having the confidence and gravitas to show off your expertise.

Start by picking a niche that you can use to showcase your skills, whether it's fashion, health and wellness, beauty or something else entirely. You can also get creative with how you present yourself—are there any topics that you can do a deep dive on? Or perhaps try live streaming product demos or tutorials?

Be sure to vary the type of content you post and experiment with different types of media like photos, videos and podcasts. Presenting yourself in different ways will not only keep things interesting but also attract people who are interested in what you have to say. And most importantly, remember to be authentic - this genuine connection is what truly makes an entrepreneur stand out.

Making Time Management Sexy

Time management isn't always seen as sexy, but it can be! When you're an entrepreneur, time is of the essence. You have to manage it wisely if you want to get things done and take your business to the next level.

Start by setting your priorities. What tasks need to get done, and which can wait? Make sure you're not trying to do too much at once, and focus on one task at a time until it's completed.

Take regular breaks throughout the day, even if they're just 5 minutes here and there. Don't forget to make time for yourself: set aside moments when you'll do something that gives you pleasure. Taking care of yourself helps ensure that your energy reserves are full and you're ready to take on the next task with enthusiasm.

Time management can be a sexy skill if you approach it with the right attitude!

Setting Goals That Turn Heads

It's no surprise that people turn their heads when you're successful. You can use this to your advantage by setting ambitious goals and dreaming big.

No matter how small the goal, it should speak to your sexiness and be something that you can be proud of. Stretching yourself gives you a sense of confidence and completed goals provide a feeling of accomplishment that make you look more attractive.

Set yourself up for success by breaking down your goals into smaller, more achievable tasks that are easy to track. Figure out what motivates you and keep a positive mindset while working towards them. Having an optimistic attitude makes it easier to stay on track and increase the chances of success—which just makes you even more attractive!

Knowing When to Ask for Help

The last but certainly not least tip of becoming the sexiest entrepreneur is to know when to ask for help. As entrepreneurs, we often want to do everything on our own, but the truth is that no one can be a master of all trades. So if there's something you need help with and you don't have the skills or time, don't be afraid to outsource it or hire someone who does.

For instance, if you're launching a new product, hiring an experienced product manager or marketer can help ensure its success. Or if you need help managing your finances better, a financial advisor may come in handy. Seek out people who are experts in their fields and willing to lend a hand—you never know what resources they can bring to the table.

Conclusion

So get to it! Unleash your inner sex symbol and attract more customers, partners, and investors with these tips. And remember, always stay true to yourself and your brand values. Sexy is as sexy does, after all.

When you exude sex appeal and confidence, people will take notice. So go out there and work hard, play hard, and show the world what you're made of. You've got this!

GET READY FOR VALENTINE'S DAY:
TIPS TO MAKE IT SEXY

It's that time of year again! The pressure is on to make Valentine's Day special for your partner. But don't worry, we're here to help. Below are some tips to help make your Valentine's Day sexy and unforgettable.

Set the Mood for Valentine's Day

You've probably seen the movies: a montage of couples getting ready for their big night. He's shaving, she's putting on her makeup, and both are looking incredibly sexy.

It's the perfect image to get you in the mood for Valentine's Day.

But don't worry if you're not quite there yet. We've got a few tips to help you set the mood and make this Valentine's Day one to remember.

First, start by turning off your phone and other electronic devices.

This is your time, and you don't want anything to interrupt it. Next, dim the lights and light some candles.

This will help create a romantic atmosphere. Finally, put on some sexy music and get ready to unleash your inner seductress.

CREATE A SEXY ATMOSPHERE WITH DELICATE LIGHTING

You don't need to go all out with the decorations and candles to set the mood. In fact, sometimes going too over-the-top can be a bit tacky. Keep it simple with some delicate lighting instead.

Candles always make a romantic setting, but this Valentine's Day, try something new and switch up the typical red and pink candles for something a little more subtle.

opting for white or cream-colored candles will create a softer, sexier atmosphere.

You can also set the mood with some strategically placed lamps or sconces. Dim the lights and watch your lover's eyes light up as they see how much effort you went to create a special evening just for them.

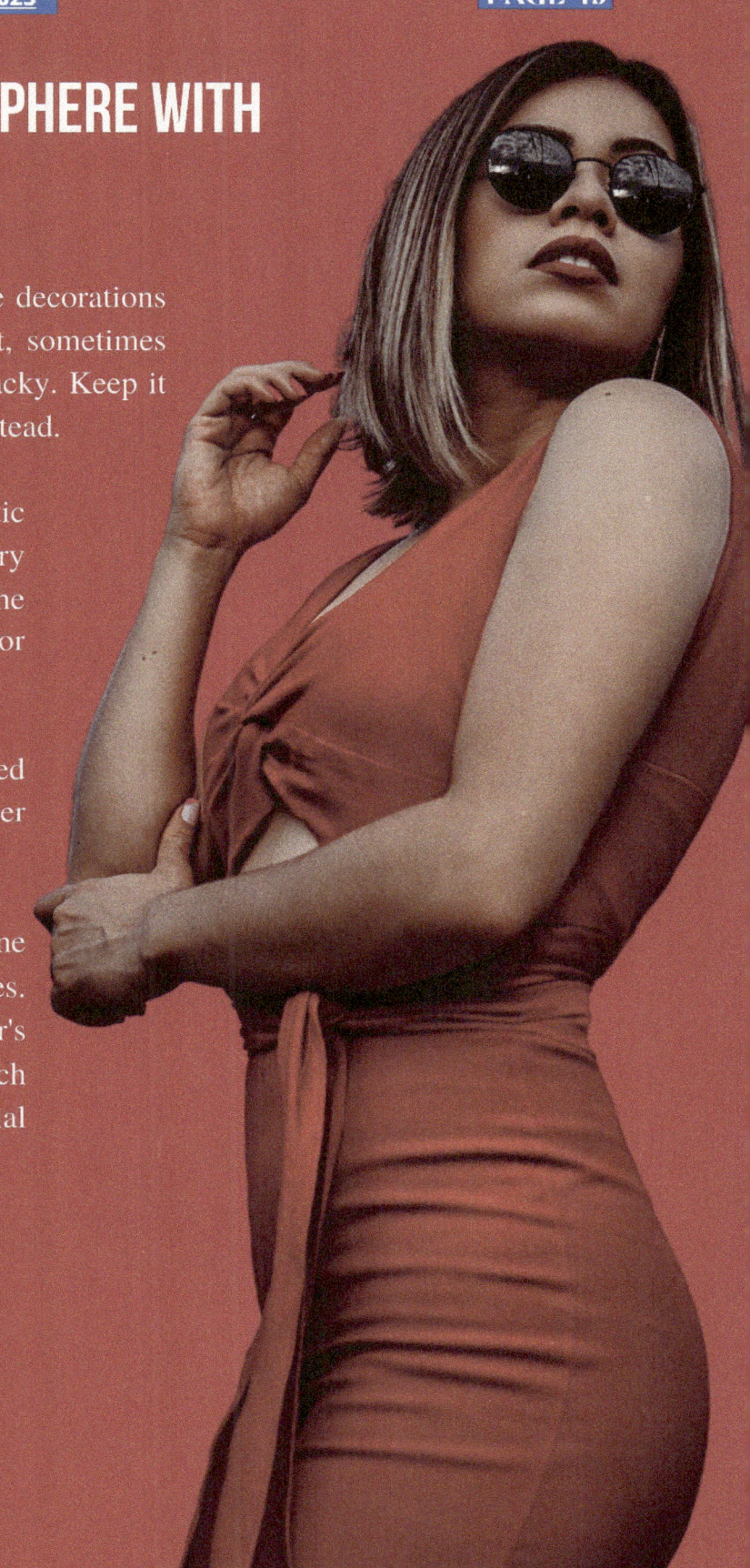

GET CREATIVE WITH YOUR OUTFIT

It's time to get creative with your outfit! This is the perfect opportunity to show your partner how much you care.

Why not try something unexpected? A little bit of lace or some sheer fabric can add a touch of sexiness to any outfit. If you're feeling really daring, maybe go for a lingerie look. But keep in mind, the most important thing is to feel comfortable and confident in what you're wearing.

Whatever you do, make sure you have fun with it! This is a special day, meant to be enjoyed.

CHOOSE A SPECIAL PLAYLIST

Setting the right atmosphere is all about picking the right music. Choose some songs that make you feel connected to each other, pick up the pace with some slower and some faster songs. You can even create your own special Valentine's Day playlist!

An alternative to a playlist is a sexy podcast to provide a little audio stimulation. Depending on what kind of mood you are going for, there are plenty of options out there for couples. From burn-it-up romance to slow and sultry, you're sure to find something to get your night off on the right foot.

Don't forget to choose some fun and appropriate background music when it's time for dinner. Maybe something romantic and melodic or something more upbeat and playful, depending on how active you want the evening to be.

The important thing is that both of you enjoy it!

PICK A SEXY LOCATION

Now it's time to turn up the heat by picking a setting that's extra special.

Think about booking a private room at a restaurant and having dinner for two. You can also check out inns and bed and breakfasts near your hometown, or Airbnb options in a romantic destination. Or go all out and take your Valentine away for a weekend getaway.

If you want to stay at home, plan an indoor picnic with all your favorite snacks, light some candles, throw on some fun music and just let the evening (and the sparks) unfold.

And if the weather permits, why not pack up a romantic dinner for two and head out to your favorite spot? Watching the sunset with your Valentine is always romantic – followed by a starry night gazing at the stars together.

BUSINESS INSIGHT MAGAZINE | ISSUE 19 | 2023 PAGE 49

ADD CREATIVE TOUCHES LIKE GIFTS AND DESSERTS

Valentine's Day is all about showing your partner you care, and there are so many creative ways to do it. Make them a personalized card, buy their favorite flowers, or get them something special to commemorate the day.

You could also make or buy them a special dessert. If you're feeling extra ambitious, whip up some homemade chocolates in fun shapes like hearts or lips. Or make something sweet for breakfast that morning like French toast with strawberries and whipped cream. A little effort goes a long way when it comes to showing your partner you care!

To get into the Valentine's Day spirit even more, why not throw on some sexy lingerie? If you don't already have any in your wardrobe, now is the perfect time to give it a try! Whether you're looking for something that's romantic or naughty, there are plenty of options out there—just make sure to pick something you feel comfortable wearing.

BUSINESS
INSIGHT MAGAZINE

ADVERTISING

WAYS TO PROMOTE YOUR BUSINESS

Since YEAR FOUNDED, we've been dedicated to crafting creative strategies that shape and ignite brand acceleration. From concept ideation to execution, BUSINESS INSIGHT MAGAZINE is here to help you every step of the way.

Business Insight Magazine can connect you to one of the United States largest audiences Advertise with Business Insight Magazine and unlock thousands of new customers, grow your business and increase profits.

Advertise in Business Insight Magazine and boost your business.

Let's get started with your ad, contact us today!

www.businessinsightmag.com

THROUGH TANTRA TO SEXOLOGY
WHY COMBINING SCIENCE WITH SPIRITUALITY ALLOWS YOU TO BETTER UNDERSTAND YOUR SEXUALITY?

It all started with tantra - a special form of meditation that combines conscious breathing, touch and shared experience. I understand this unique form of working with the body as learning to give and receive intimacy, intimate communication, allowing to achieve a special kind of understanding with a partner. Its benefits can be defined both in psychological and spiritual terms - thanks to it you will work on accepting yourself and what happens to you.

We live in difficult times - first the pandemic and isolation, now the war - I perfectly understand why my clients struggle with various problems in relationships. Hence, I decided on a rather unusual form of help - in my workshop I combine sexology with spirituality. I am convinced that these two fields do not have to be mutually exclusive. I believe that it is definitely better to combine than divide, and thanks to the synergy effect, my patients rediscover their sexuality and experience it in an increasingly conscious way! I will also add that the study of sexuality is an interdisciplinary field in itself, so tantra can be a perfect complement!

workshop I combine sexology with spirituality. I am convinced that these two fields do not have to be mutually exclusive. I believe that it is definitely better to combine than divide, and thanks to the synergy effect, my patients rediscover their sexuality and experience it in an increasingly conscious way! I will also add that the study of sexuality is an interdisciplinary field in itself, so tantra can be a perfect complement!

What exactly is an encounter with tantra and spirituality?

Spirituality is the higher dimension of our psyche - all other spheres of human life integrate on this level. It helps us answer questions about the meaning of life and leads us to actively seek answers to the questions the Universe asks us. Meeting with tantra is really a meeting with yourself - your emotions, corporeality and spirituality that each of us has. During this extraordinary experience, you open up to new ones, saying goodbye to old ways of understanding the world. In its original form, it was a religious and philosophical trend originating from India and Tibet, but today the practice takes place without any religious structure. You begin to build your consciousness anew, which is based on boundless love for yourself and others. You start to create your own reality devoid of prejudices and unsupportive patterns.

All the workshops I took part in were an extraordinary experience for me, during which I felt as if I had been born again. The organizers paid special attention to making all participants feel safe - this element is extremely important, so I will mention it later. Thanks to such practices, you open up to your emotions and sexuality - you start to feel them much stronger and you realize their extraordinary power. Many people describe that thanks to tantra they understood what love really is and what it is often confused with. There is talk of the wildness of love and even its magical aspects. A particularly unique moment is the understanding that in society love is sometimes confused with lust.

It is worth noting that for each of us a meeting with tantra can be something different - we differ from each other in terms of mental properties and have had different experiences. Such diversity in spiritual practices is extraordinary, because thanks to this we can learn
from each other! Tantra is suitable for everyone - all you need is willingness and openness - it doesn't matter how old you are! I often call tantra a meeting of bodies, hearts and souls, because the
energy in the form of love fills our entire body and mind! Every, even the smallest element of you becomes important and radiates pure love!

While acknowledging it, you will transgress in many areas - enlightenment, building longer lasting, more conscious relationships, and a richer sex life. People are different from each other, they are at different moments in their lives, so what the clients takes with them depends to a large extent on themselves!

How do I use tantra in working with other people?

While working with clients, I teach them to be mindful of themselves and the other person - this is an inseparable element of all spiritual practices. We talk about emotions, I often explain why they are inseparable from sexuality and should not be ashamed of them. During the session, I pay clients' attention to their carnality - I teach them how to enjoy their sexuality and show how to open up to intimacy and the needs of both themselves and their partner. How to take care of your boundaries and not cross the boundaries of the other
person. People come to me with various problems - lack of communication in a relationship, sexual frustration, not being noticed by the other person. I am open to cooperation with everyone, because I believe that we all deserve a successful sex life. It happens that people who come to me do not see any chance to improve the situation. Sometimes they lack motivation for deeper changes in the form of psychotherapy and want to try something more ad hoc. Sometimes they confuse the need for intimacy with a woman with a sexual need. Sometimes my clients have a

successful sex life, but they want to open up to something new - each of these approaches is perfectly fine and I approach each individually. Thanks to tantra, I have become even more open to the needs of others, which allows me to better listen to the needs of other people. I believe that the combination of tantra and classic coaching allows you to enter a different dimension of corporeality and sexual awareness - this is how my clients come up with unconventional solutions on their own.

Tantra concerns the area of our sexuality - it can be both a one-off experience and a long- term path of development - each individual decides which path is closer to him! In my work, I combine theory with practice - I pass on knowledge related to sexology, while encouraging my clients to experiment and play themselves. I believe that the combination of the assumptions of Taoism, psychology and bodywork can bring surprising results!

Sources of knowledge and inspiration

My interest in sexology began in 2010 - this sub-discipline of psychology deals with human sexual needs, as well as proper development in this sphere. He also pays special attention to understanding his emotions and expressing them correctly.

I constantly emphasize that work is also my passion, thanks to which my actions become more effective. I deeply believe that learning and improving one's competences can become
a pleasure in itself!

I graduated from psychology studies with a specialization in clinical psychology. However, I have always been drawn to spirituality, so I decided to take a one-year course in transpersonal psychology. During various workshops, I learnt the secrets of altered states of consciousness and mystical experiences.

I have participated in many tantric massage courses, and I have been going to tantric
reunions every year for several years! Exploring this knowledge gives me great pleasure, because I learn something new every time, which allows me to work more effectively with clients! I am constantly developing my competences, which is why I am currently finishing another faculty in the field of sexology. Exploring this subject gives me a lot of satisfaction and I am

convinced that I have more than one training ahead of me. I was involved in courses at the Sex Positive Institute, which opened me even more to sexual diversity and difference - I understood what exactly this phenomenon is and how I can pass this knowledge and acceptance to others. Inclusivity, sexual education, gender identity - these are also what I share during my sessions.

I took part in intimacy coaching trainings, thanks to which I also disseminate my knowledge about setting boundaries and assertively saying.

Everything I have learned I pass on to my clients because I believe that only consensual sex can be a great experience!

I encourage everyone to discover themselves as an independent being. I run a blog and am active on social media. During each session, I encourage you to open up to your freedom and experience it as fully as possible. I am constantly improving my competences, which is why I am currently finishing another faculty in the field of sexology. Exploring this subject gives me a lot of satisfaction and I am convinced that there are many more courses ahead of me!

I also believe that academic learning does not have to be the only source of knowledge - I go to Tantra Festivals in Poland and around the world. Thanks to such trips, I have the opportunity to meet many interesting people with similar views. I strongly believe that experience allows you to accept diversity and open up to other people!

What should you pay special attention to when practicing tantra?

As a coach, I pay special attention to where I get my knowledge from, because I care about the well-being of my clients. The basic principle in working with other people is to do no harm - this motto is sacred to me.

If you want to start an adventure with spiritual practices, the right space and people from whom you gain knowledge are very important. Don't worry - such practices are by no means dangerous, but if you want to make the most of them, you should take care of a few things.

Remember to choose a place where you feel confident and know that nothing will disturb your peaceful experience. If you

decide to practice with someone, make sure it is someone you trust. I run workshops during which I show how to practice tantra and derive pleasure from contact both with oneself and with another person. I pay attention to where to start - I show how to
take care of your mental comfort, teach communication in sexual relationships and talk about your needs and boundaries to another person.

I am happy that my work is also my passion - the satisfaction of my clients gives me great satisfaction - a smile on their faces and a calm body. I love sharing my knowledge with others, especially if I can help someone! I encourage everyone to find out more about tantra because, as I mentioned, all you need is openness. I am also fascinated by how people experience such practices - everyone draws something from this experience and thus becomes richer!

We all deserve a successful sex life because sex is one of our basic needs.
My work is a perfect example that spirituality and science can go hand in hand, and thanks to this my clients can achieve more lasting effects of working on themselves!

Tantra can be something that will change your life forever! Perhaps you feel stuck in apathy and are looking for a new path in life? Maybe opening up to new experiences is what you need right now? I have already helped many people in crisis - life writes different scenarios, and the difficult emotions accompanying them should be treated as a hint for the future. I always say that what is difficult in life can become a unique opportunity for us to develop! My clients often describe the meeting with me as a breakthrough event in their lives, thanks to which they opened up more to themselves and experienced emotions that they have long forgotten or never felt. They became more attentive to both their own and the other person emotions. They learned how to deal with them and how to safely communicate about their needs. Their attitude towards the world also changed, because they began to see it as a place full of love that you have to learn to share!

Each of us is a causative being responsible for our actions and thoughts. Everyone has the right to full happiness and love - its never too late to open up to change!

JEWELZ YOGA llc

Ready to assist you achieving your body goals

Workout With

JEWEL

Professional Yoga Trainer

BOOK MORE SESSIONS
SAVE MORE MONEY

Feel free to contact me with any questions or inquiries.
Join Jewelz Yoga tribe by joining one of many individual, group, personalized to your event and specialty yoga classes.

Together we will make the world a more beautiful place...
one yoga breath at a time

JEWELZYOGA@GMAIL.COM

Make Appointment
www.jewelzyoga.com

SCENT THAT MAKES YOU MORE ELEGANT

BOMBSHELL

EAU DE PARFUM

Bold & Iconic

Sparkling and fresh, our number-one fragrance is a timeless mix of fresh-cut exotic flowers and afternoon sun.

Purple Passion Fruit • Shangri-la Peony
Vanilla Orchid

SCAN ME

CPSIA information can be obtained
at www.ICGtesting.com
Printed in the USA
BVHW012048100323
660179BV00016B/808

9 798211 542112